MW00804777

Signature Solos

9 All-New Piano Solos by Favorite Alfred Composers

Selected and edited by **Gayle Kowalchyk**

Students love getting new music, and teachers love teaching it! What could be more fun than a book of new solos by several favorite Alfred composers? This collection of piano solos was expressly written for the *Signature Solos* series. A variety of different musical styles is found in each of the books.

As editor of this collection, it was a joy for me to play through many solos to find just the right grouping of pieces for each book. I looked for appealing sounds while considering the technical and musical abilities of students at each level. Students are sure to enjoy playing these "signature solos" for friends and family, informally or on recitals.

Gayle Kowalchyk

Alfred Music
P.O. Box 10003
Van Nuys, CA 91410-0003
alfred.com

ISBN-10: 1-4706-3215-2
ISBN-13: 978-1-4706-3215-1

Cover Photo
Colored Pencils: © iStock. / Adam Smigielski

Looking Through the Mist

Robert D. Vandall

Very flexible and expressive

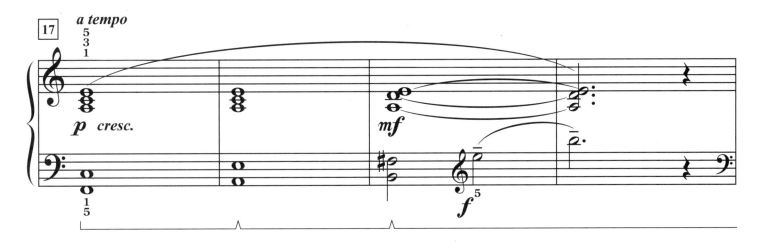

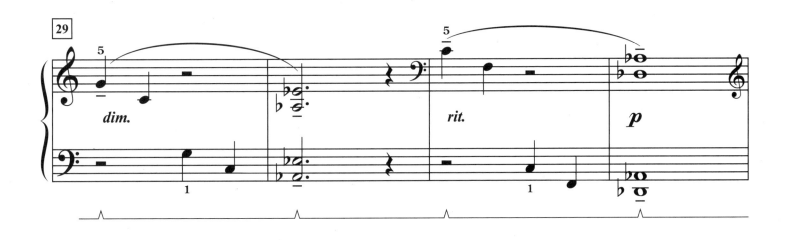

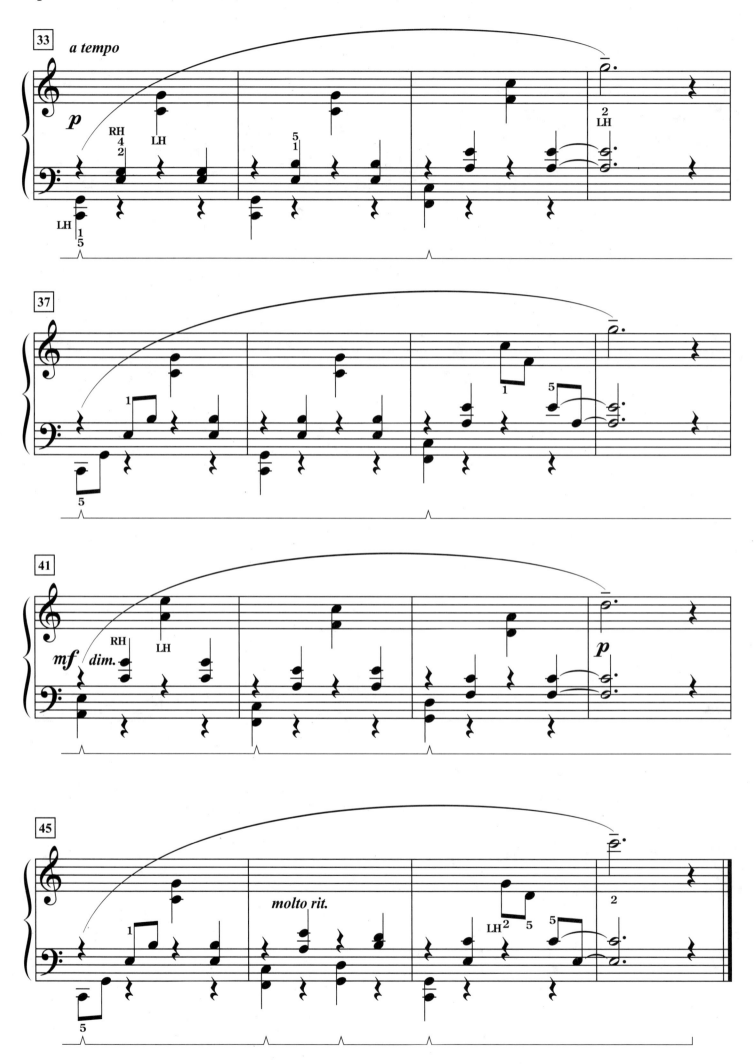

Mystery of the Black Diamond

Wynn-Anne Rossi

Mysteriously

Stomp!

Kathy Holmes

Jazz Riff

Melody Bober

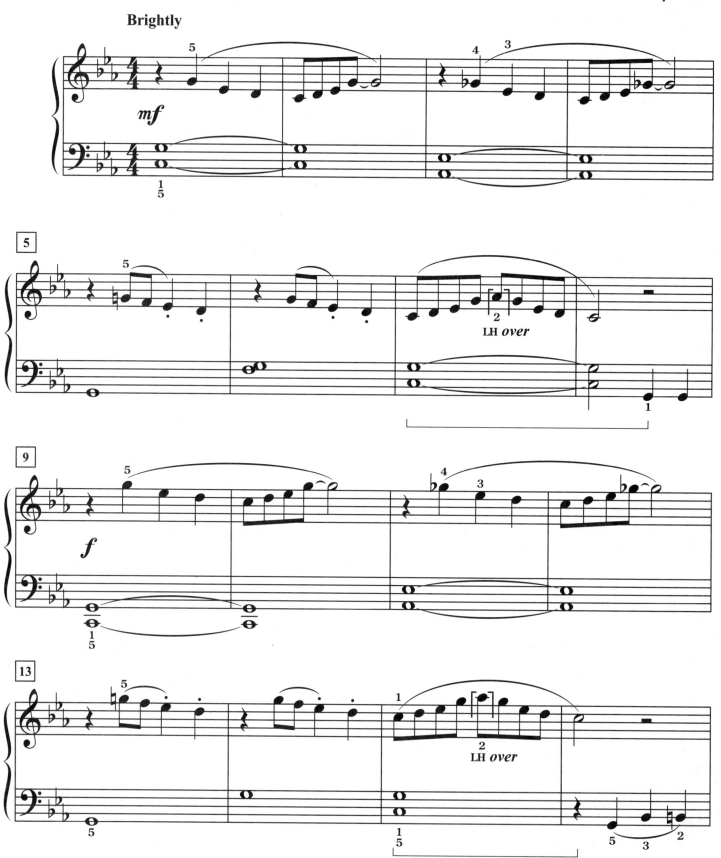

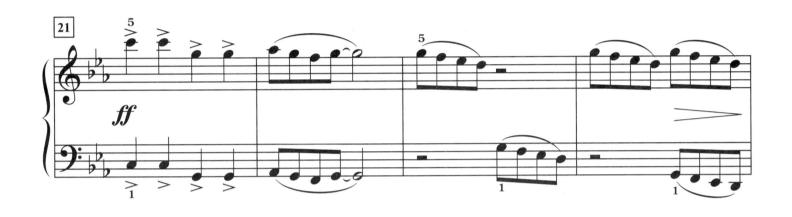

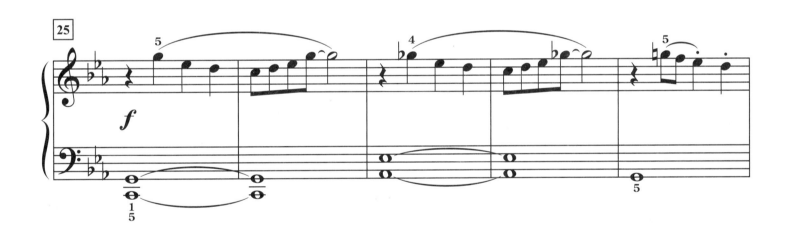

Cloud Forests

Ted Cooper

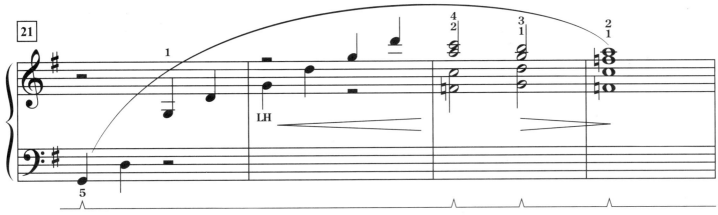

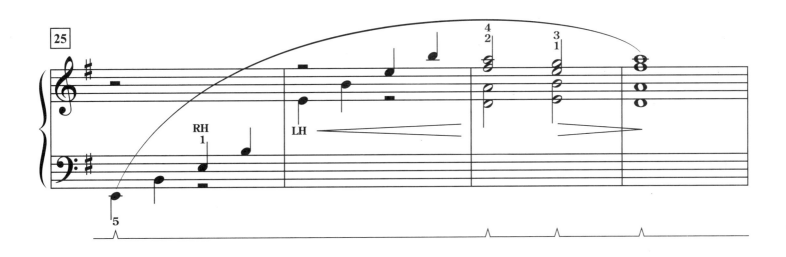

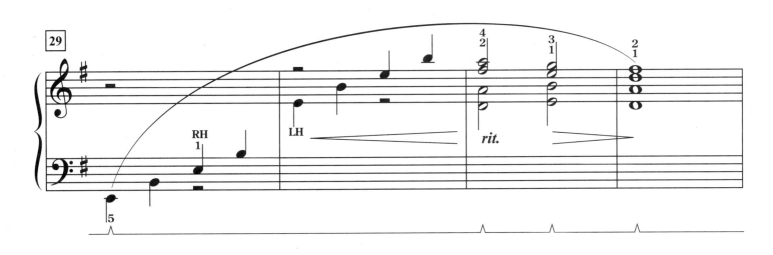

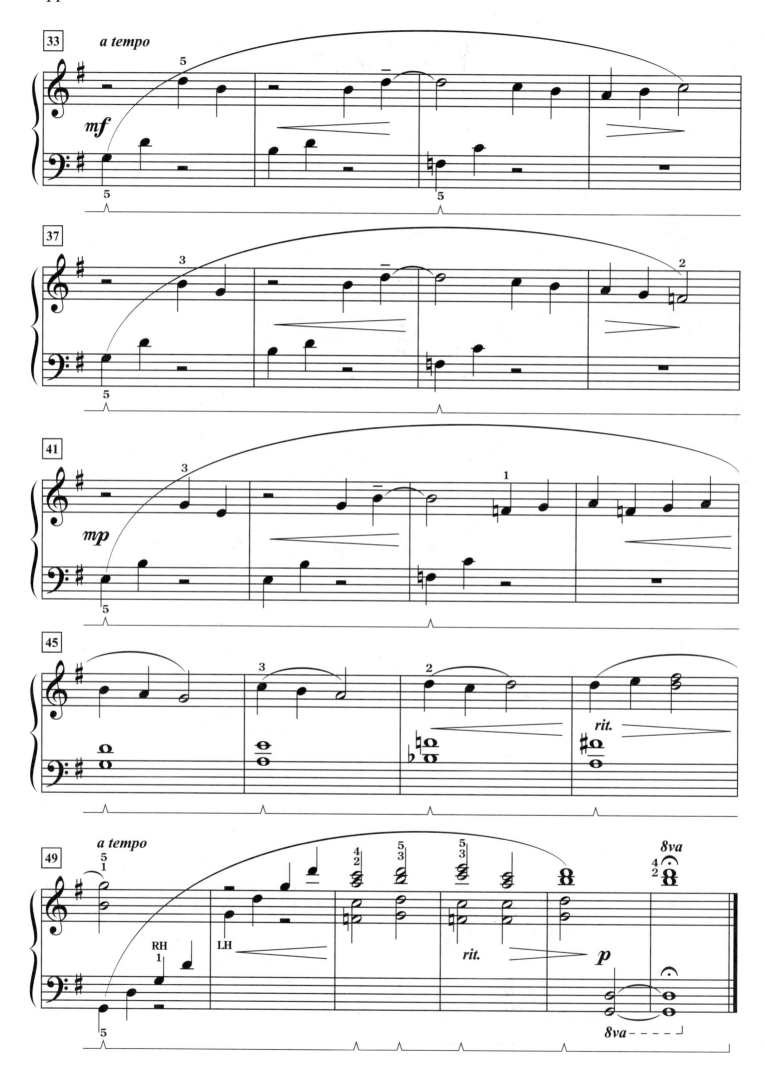

Outfoxed!

W.T. Skye Garcia

19 *Foxes at play...*

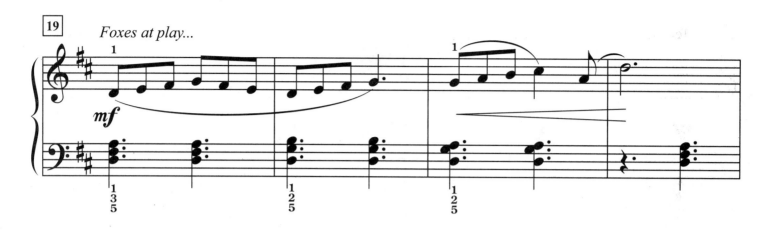

23

Slower

27 *Crossing a stream...*

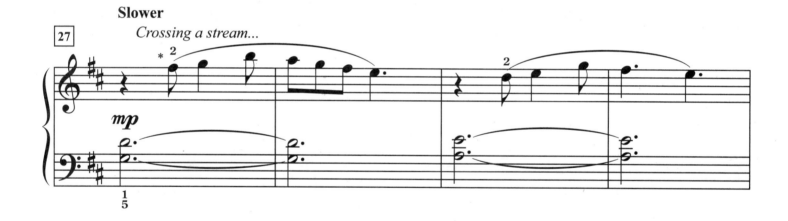

31

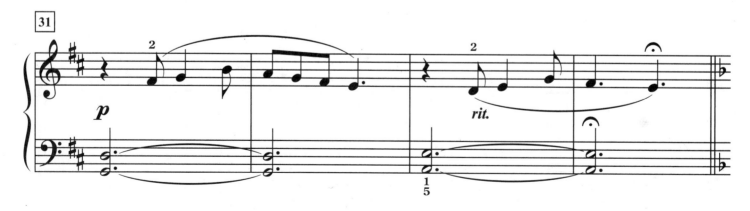

* Based on a theme from Beethoven's Sixth (Pastorale) Symphony, a theme
that he associated with "cheerful feelings upon arrival in the country."

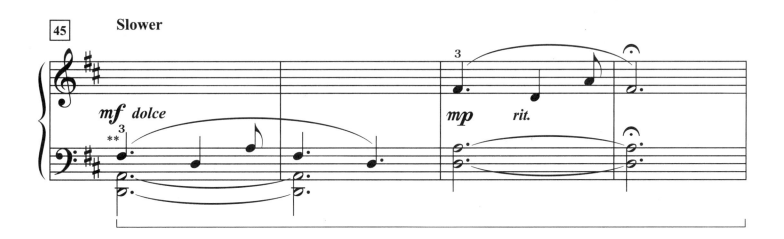

** Beethoven said of this theme (also from his Sixth Symphony) that
it represented "Happy and thankful feelings after the storm."

Dance of the Gypsies

Martha Mier

Nocturne

Ted Cooper

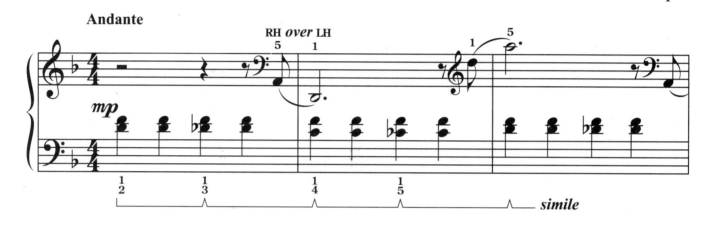

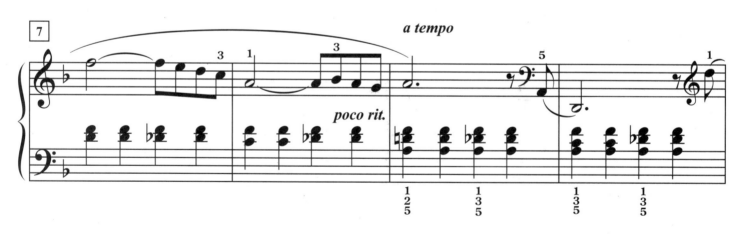

Dedicated to the piano students of Linda Kennedy in Maumelle, Arkansas

New Day

Chris Goldston

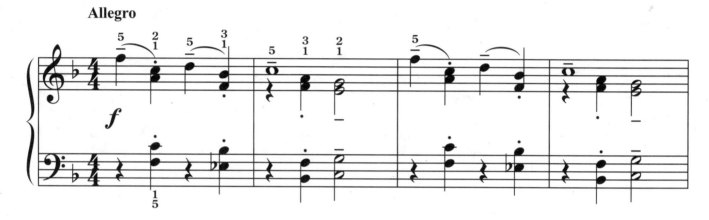

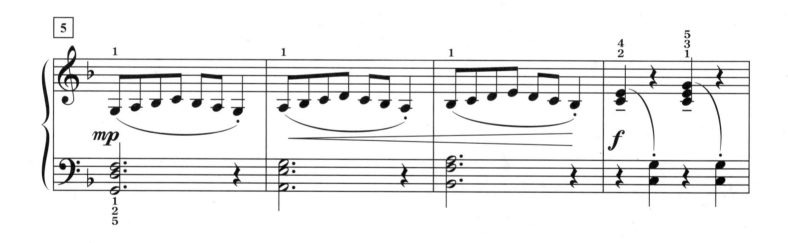